I Want To Be A Dancer

Written by LaTeria Jordan

I Want to Be A Dancer
By: Lateria Jordan
Copyright © 2017 by Dr. Lateria Jordan

ISBN: 978-0-9989239-0-1

Published by True Vine Publishing Company
P.O. Box 22448
Nashville, TN. 37218
www.TrueVinePublishing.org

Illustrated by Najwa Jai

All rights reserved. No part of this book may be reproduced or transmitted in any form or by any means, electronic or mechanical, including photocopying, recording or by any information storage and retrieval system, without written permission from the author, except for the inclusion of brief quotations in a review.

Printed in the United States of America—First Print

WRITTEN BY DR. LATERIA JORDAN
ILLUSTRATIONS BY NAJWA JAI

I would like to dedicate this book to my niece Marrari Tucker.
Marrari became a ballerina at the age of three.
She was the inspiration for this
book because she loves dancing and music just like I did when I was a little girl.

I would also like to dedicate this book to my college dance
coordinator of Tennessee State University,
Ms. Judy F. Gentry. She trained me and pushed me beyond my own expectations.

Lastly, I want to thank my mother Wanda Tucker who has inspired
me and given me unconditional love.
Special thanks to Najwa Jai, the artist and illustrator of *I Want to be a Dancer*.

Dance Terms

I want to be a Dancer....

1. Rond de Jambe [rän də 'ZHämb] - A circular movement of the leg that can be performed on the ground or during a jump.

2. Plié [plē'ā] - A movement in which a dancer bends the knees and straightens them again, usually with the feet turned out and heels firmly on the ground.

3. Releve [relə'vā] - A movement in which the dancer rises on the tips of the toes.

4. Tendu [tän'do͞o] - The action of stretching your leg and foot out from one position to another, while keeping it on the floor.

5. Fouette [fo͞oə'tā] - A pirouette performed with a circular whipping movement of the raised leg to the side.

6. Attitude [adə.t(y)ood] - A position where the dancer is standing on one leg with the other lifted, usually to the front (devant) or back (derrière).

7. Chasse [Sa-shay] - A movement in which one foot extends forward, and the back foot then "chases" and meets up with the front for a quick moment before the front foot shoots forward again, all while traveling forward.

8. Pirouette [pirə'wet] - An act of spinning on one foot, typically with the raised foot touching the knee of the supporting leg.

9. Grand Battement [gräN bät'mäN] - A movement in which both legs are kept straight and one leg is kicked outward from the body and in again.

10. Arabesque [erə'besk] - A posture in which the body is supported on one 4leg, with the other leg extended horizontally backward.

11. Pointe [point/pwant] - Dance performed on the tips of the toes.

12. Pointe shoes- The shoes that ballerinas wear to be safely supported and dance on the tips of their toes in classical and contemporary ballet.

I want to be a dancer, and I'm 6 years old.
My name is Mari, and this is how my story goes.
I dance for pleasure, pretty in pink,
shake my head, and tap my feet.

I want to be a dancer, and stand on my toes,
like the ballerinas on T.V. with tutus and bows.
I watch very closely as the ballerinas smile,
their partners spin them around and around.
They're lifted in the air, light as a feather;
Then gracefully bow as the crowd reverences their presence.

I want to be a dancer like my sister in dance class;
She dances around, prances, and laughs.
As she dances and moves, she's filled with joy,
because she knows her debut routine is a performance
the audience will enjoy!

She leaps real high like a frog in a pond,
then she lands real soft like a gliding swan.
"Rond de Jambe" her teacher says,
as she tries real hard to make circles with her legs.

I want to be a dancer,

my mommy signs me up too;

I learn to *Plié* and *Relevé* in my pink ballet shoes.

I am a beginner, so I learn the technique

Of being graceful with good posture and soft on my feet.

I want to be a dancer so I pretend when at home.
I watch in the mirror as I turn on my toes.
I put on my leotard, leg warmers, and tights,
then I dance around to music and pretend all night.
I bow to my audience that's not really there,
so when my dream comes true
I'll already be prepared.

I want to be a dancer, I learn to *Tendu*,

in first and second position, I flex my pink dance shoes.

I dance around like nobody is there,

then I see my silhouette as I laugh at it's glare.

My sister then tries to teach me a, *Fouetté* she

holds my arms high and twirls me as I rotate.

I want to be a dancer, and learn even more,
Attitude and gracefulness as I *Chasse* on the dance floor.
I learn to do a *Pirouette* with the bar as my guide;
I use my momentum to rotate and turn again clockwise.

I want to be a dancer, and kick high in the air,
"Grand Battement" my teacher said as I extend my leg.
I have more Attitude and becoming more poised
and polished, just like a new blossomed flower.

I want to be a dancer, so I tried an Arabesque
I fell on my derrière and all my friends laughed.
"Mari" they asked, "why do you practice all the time?"
I said "practice makes perfect, and
dancing is how I shine".

I want to be a dancer, so I dream about it at night,
as I leap high in the sky while the moon shines bright.
I even dream of tap dancing on the moon,
and touching the stars because dancing is my muse.

I want to be a dancer and it's time for the recital.
My parents take pictures as I grin with excitement.
I bow like the "big girls" as they receive their roses,
then we all grab hands and walk off on our toes.

I am finally a dancer and I move on to Ballet II.
My teacher told me I'm going to need Pointe shoes.
Practice makes perfect and I'll get better with time.
In a few years, I'll be a soloist at the recital,
and the stage will be all mine.

BALLET WORD SEARCH

```
R E L E V E U C R X P B
I I X F O U E T T E L C
X H B P O I N T E Z I H
A T T I T U D E N D E A
D A R A B E S Q U E K S
U K H F O D T E N D U S
P O I N T E S H O E S E
N D P I R O U E T T E T
```

LET'S COLOR!

WORD SCRAMBLE

| A | N | D | E | R | C |

| I | E | P | L |

| B | L | A | L | T | E |

| U | T | T | U |

About the Author

LaTeria Jordan is a graduate from Tennessee State University with a B.S. in Speech Pathology and Audiology and a M.Ed. in Special Education. She recently graduated in the Spring of 2019 with her Ed.D in Curriculum and Instruction. LaTeria values education and believes that knowledge is endless.

She has served as a special educator in the states of TN, GA, and CA over the past 19 years. She has 15 years of experience coaching and mentoring dance lines/majorettes, and other auxiliary squads. She has always been passionate about dance and the arts. This passion is why she chose to write the inspirational story of "I want to be a Dancer" to share with all little girls who have a love for dance—especially girls of color.

Although education and teaching are important to her, she has always found joy in mentoring the youth. She realizes one of her purposes in life is to share with young people the significance of aligning their talents and passions to their career interest. Although she knew her passions early on, she didn't have assurance to truly pursue them. She is now confident enough to finally share these artistic gifts with her community.

This book "I want to be a Dancer" is her first book in a series of children's books. The next projects to be completed is "I want to be an Architect" and later "I want to be a Teacher". . LaTeria is asking that all her readers, family, and friends continue to support her efforts as a writer. She is also praying that by the grace of God, she's able to catapult her writing into a full-time career, so she can continue to share stories and inspire.

WRITTEN BY DR. LATERIA JORDAN
ILLUSTRATIONS BY NAJWA JAI

www.ingramcontent.com/pod-product-compliance
Lightning Source LLC
Chambersburg PA
CBHW041439010526
44118CB00002B/123